Sweethearts of Rhythm

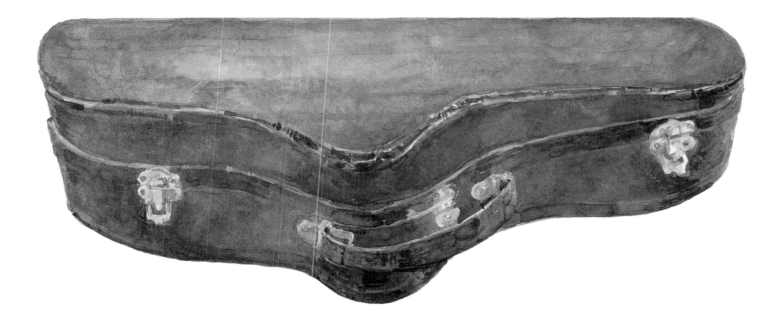

Sweethearts of Rhythm

THE STORY OF THE GREATEST ALL-GIRL SWING BAND IN THE WORLD

WRITTEN BY

MARILYN NELSON

ILLUSTRATED BY

JERRY PINKNEY

DIAL BOOKS

AN IMPRINT OF PENGUIN GROUP (USA) INC.

DIAL BOOKS
An imprint of Penguin Group (USA) Inc.
Published by The Penguin Group
Penguin Group (USA) Inc., 375 Hudson Street, New York, NY 10014, U.S.A.
Penguin Group (Canada), 90 Eglinton Avenue East, Suite 700, Toronto, Ontario, Canada M4P 2Y3 (a division of Pearson Penguin Canada Inc.)
Penguin Books Ltd, 80 Strand, London WC2R 0RL, England
Penguin Ireland, 25 St. Stephen's Green, Dublin 2, Ireland (a division of Penguin Books Ltd)
Penguin Group (Australia), 250 Camberwell Road, Camberwell, Victoria 3124, Australia (a division of Pearson Australia Group Pty Ltd)
Penguin Books India Pvt Ltd, 11 Community Centre, Panchsheel Park, New Delhi - 110 017, India
Penguin Group (NZ), 67 Apollo Drive, Rosedale, North Shore 0632, New Zealand (a division of Pearson New Zealand Ltd)
Penguin Books (South Africa) (Pty) Ltd, 24 Sturdee Avenue, Rosebank, Johannesburg 2196, South Africa
Penguin Books Ltd, Registered Offices: 80 Strand, London WC2R 0RL, England

The author would like to acknowledge the journals in which some of these poems first appeared: Margie, Mi Poesias, Pluck!, and Redivider.
With gratitude also to Lauri Hornik, Pamela Espeland, Mel Nelson, and Tim Moran for their helpful suggestions, and to Wynton Marsalis for less direct guidance.

Photograph on page 75 courtesy of Frank Driggs

Designed by Lily Malcom
Text set in Exotic 350
Manufactured in China

Library of Congress Cataloging-in-Publication Data

Nelson, Marilyn, date.
Sweethearts of Rhythm : the story of the greatest all-girl swing band
in the world / Marilyn Nelson ; illustrated by Jerry Pinkney.
p. cm.
ISBN 978-0-8037-3187-5
1. International Sweethearts of Rhythm—Poetry. 2. International
Sweethearts of Rhythm—Juvenile literature. 3. Women jazz
musicians—United States—Poetry. 4. Women jazz musicians—United
States—Biography—Juvenile literature. 5. Big bands—United
States—History—20th century. I. Pinkney, Jerry, ill. II. Title.
PS3573.A4795S94 2009
811'.54—dc22
[B]
2008046255

The full-color artwork was prepared using graphite, color pencil, watercolor and collage.

To Malia and Sasha Obama,

their dreams, and the dreams of other young women of their generation.

May the music continue. — M.N.

To Jessye Norman, whose voice has lifted our hearts and moved our spirits. — J.P.

Galvanizing

Nina de la Cruz on Tenor Sax
Ina Belle Byrd, Judy Bayron, and Helen Jones on Trombone

With a twilit velvet musky tone
as the pawnshop door is locked,
an ancient tenor saxophone
spins off a riff of talk.

"A thousand thousand gigs ago,
when I was just second-hand,"
it says, "I spent my glory years
on the road with an all-girl band."

From a shelf in the corner, three trombones
bray in unison: They say
they, too, were played in a gals' swing band
way back in the day.

Then effortlessly, a blues in C
arises out of a phrase
and the old hocked instruments find the groove
and swing of the Good Old Days.

I Can't Get Started

Edna Williams on Accordion
Yvonne Plummer on Bagpipes

On our church-to-church fund-raising tours of the South
for the Piney Woods Country Life School,
we were the instruments who had the most breath,
and we were handled with consummate skill.

If only the girls had been paid a fair wage;
if only their musicianship had been less confined,
they might not have run away in righteous rage,
leaving us, by accident, behind.

Bugle Call Rag

Nova Lee McGee on Trumpet

No trumpet has ever been tempted
not to funambulate
on the filament of a melody.
We're all stars; we were made for the limelight.

I was bought second-hand in Biloxi.
(I'd been honorably discharged by the Army band.)
I moaned, seeing this as a step down:
to be played by a woman: I, who'd been played by a real man.

But the first time we stepped out front and center
and blasted the rafters with a long-held E,
I knew that all those years of playing marches
had kept me from being all I was meant to be.

Chattanooga Choo-Choo

Twin Ione or Irene Gresham on Tenor Sax

Some days the earth seems to reverse its spin,
and everyone seems to be flailing around in the dark.
The day war was declared, one of the twins
unpacked me for practice as usual, and set to work.

She performed the daily ritual of the reed—
soaking the reed, trimming it, fitting it in,
tightening the ligature. She bowed her head,
then lifted me and eased me into song.

She was pushing herself through me to an open space
where people can be one.

It was "Chattanooga Choo-Choo," but it was a prayer for peace.
She was trying to change the world through sound.

Jump, Jump, Jump

Helen Saine on Alto Sax

From ballroom to ballroom, the unsleeping eye of Jim Crow
ever upon us, we traveled the United States
of colored America, bouncing on back-country roads
and gliding on highways. At picnics, we practiced our charts,
our polished brass gleaming. We welcomed farm children who ran
one or two miles to be able to listen and dance.

> *Do you want to jump, children?*
> —Yeah!
> *Do you want to jump, children?*
> —Yeah!

Domestics, farm laborers, new hires in factory jobs;
the Apollo, the Royal, the Regal, and the Cotton Club,
redolent of Dixie-Peach pomade and Ivory soap,
they jumped 'til the stars disappeared and the roosters woke up.

It Don't Mean a Thing

Pauline Braddy on Drums

On some tunes, she'd lash my bass home like a jockey;
on some all she did was high-hat tickle the beat,
always gracefully making the transitions,
watching the music and the dancers' feet.
The jitterbug was one way people forgot
the rapidly spreading prairie fires of war.
Man, the house would bounce when her licks were hot!
We gave those people what they were dancing for.

The Hard Luck Blues

Roxanna Lucas on Guitar

From a battered, sticker-plastered case
arose a muffled chord:
"So the Sweethearts gig was glorious,
but please, don't go overboard.

"My hoboing days were glorious, too:
when I rambled, riding the rails,
playing ballads and talking blues
in boxcars and roadside camps, in jails.

"Sure, you must have had fun in the girls' swing band,
but what could that dance music say
to the farmers who'd recently seen their land
dry to dust, and blow away?

"I was still playing 'The Hard Luck Blues'
while you watched people jitterbug.
That you were 'swinging' is not a sufficient excuse.
Denial is a powerful drug."

Take the 'A' Train

Ernestine "Tiny" Davis on Trumpet

Every swing tune tells a story without words:
the truth of people breathing in unison,
the democracy of harmonies and chords,
unique, disparate voices raised as one.

I led the band in an artillery
of wittily syncopated quarter notes,
or with the buttery longing her strong lips drew from me
until a warbling April morning filled my throat!

Hey, a little forgetfulness was a good thing,
a respite from the battle-to-battle news.
The ultimate give-and-take is right there in swing:
the improvised melodic objective of jazz.

Whose music is "truer"? Your bald-eyed protest songs,
or the waves of joy in which people drowned their despair?
Forgetfulness, or a recitation of wrongs?
Shoot, taking the 'A' train was a form of prayer.

She's Crazy with the Heat

Helen Jones, Ina Bell Byrd, and Judy Jones on Trombone

Yeah. You have to hearken to the story behind each song.
That's essential to every good trombone player's art.
To articulate a note, let alone to swing,
trombone players have to feel, and to play from the heart.

So you know the seven positions. That's not enough.
You have to place the notes precisely, so they paint
a picture: bright or dark tones, smooth or rough.
Good trombonists play all over the instrument.

Yeah, the trombone section, in identical gabardine suits,
like dark Betty Grable Rosie the Riveters,
felt their way, tune after tune, to the absolute
unchanging fable of the universe:

That good exists, that love prevails over fear,
that hate and war are eventually kenneled again.
Yeah, our music told this story, to all who could hear.
Yeah: Love will prevail. Yeah. (Don't ask us when.)

Lady, Be Good

Roz Cron on Tenor Sax

My girl ran away from home with a suitcase and me
to play in a band whose musicians were a beautiful scale
of browns. They were women whom music was making free.
My favorite story happened when my girl learned how to *wail.*

In the band, she explored my range: voluptuous, fiery.
Her playing began to take on new rhythmic contours;
her spontaneous improvisations invented new stories,
melodic and nuanced portraits of love, war, and loss.

She wore thick pancake makeup, to darken her face,
and she patted on powder whenever the band took a break.
The laws of the South prohibited groups of mixed race,
and she hoped no one would notice that she was a fake:

that she was passing for colored, following swing music to its soul.
That she was shaping my pearls with the fingerprints of her groove.
That she was learning to *take a Boston,* to *get off,* to heal
the tenderest longings, strengthen the last hope of love.

On the night in question, when my girl really learned to *wail,*
after her solo, she wiped her sweaty face with her sleeve.
In those days, blacks and whites playing together risked jail.
Her white forehead glittered through, and some fool notified the police.

She was *wailing,* all right. And it led to a narrow escape!
She jumped in a cab with me, and we sped to the train.
We met up with the rest of the band on the tour's next stop.
She had to promise never to work up a sweat again!

Red-Hot Mama

"Tiny" Davis on Trumpet

My gal could sweet you to death with her beautiful tone,
then pull you out of yourself to get up and move,
body and soul propelled to a higher plane:
the body to jitterbug, the soul to something like love.

They were rationing food in those days. Every house
with a sunny yard had a "victory" vegetable plot.
My gal washed and ironed (fifty cents a blouse)
and sold sandwiches, to keep herself afloat.

Because times was hard. But all she had to do was blow,
and people of every hue and every age
got caught in a vibration that started with a tapping toe
and rapidly grew into an irresistible urge.

Was part of the population held in internment camps?
Was there a guy you hadn't heard from since before D-Day?
Let the rhythm rule your butt, let the rhythm rule your feet and limbs.
Let yourself acquiesce completely to the music of joy!

Black and Tan Fantasy

Johnnie May Rice on Guitar

It was solace, then, that swing music gave those crowds?
You and your sweethearts were really "soldiers of music,"
living like tumbleweed, bathless and underpaid,
to uplift the nation's fallen morale with acoustics?

Were you generating resilience as you played
that bouncy rhythm defined by its trill-filled time?
Was an antidote found, in jitterbugging like mad,
to the middle of the century defined by progress and crime?

Was it democratic music, making every toe tap
and every heart lift toward courage again, over fear?
Was it music more of *transcendence* than of *escape*:
each tune a tiny little victory over war?

I see. So every swing band, without speaking its name,
sort of thumbed America's nose at the threat of fascism?
Swing music wasn't half as vapid as it seemed!
You were bringing the madman down, just by swinging the rhythm!

I'm in the Mood for Swing

Willie Mae Wong on Baritone Sax

If I could have been uncurved and laid extended
length by length by my little Sweetheart's side,
one might have suspected our twinning was intended
to create the smiling impression our appearance made.

She lugged me, like a grown-up-sized infant, from place to place
(her strength was XL, though she was a 2 petite).
Carrying her handbag, her suitcase, and me in my case,
she trip-tripped around on dainty high-heeled feet.

Should I apologize if we "only" made people dance?
That one is *alive* is an adequate reason to sing!
Must beauty apologize for simple elegance?
Shoot, we didn't need a "philosophy" to swing!

THAT MAN of MINE

"TINY" DAVIS ON TRUMPET

MUSICIANS walk a tightrope. Below them lie madness and beauty.
The world was aflame, the men soldiering at the front.
The Sweethearts had no philosophy: They just did their duty.
A girl has to trumpet down Jericho, if a man can't.
A girl must fling ecstasy over the world's desperation
with flowery solos, with intricately scattered grace notes,
with hep-cat audacity. She must play a balm for her nation,
with nuanced bravado.
                                    Traversing the United States
performing one-nighters, traveling thousands of miles in a year:
the gals had a mission, expressible only in tones.
My gal could quote Satchmo so people stopped dancing to cheer.
Something powerful happened when she and I stepped out alone.
Her pristine technique wove a shimmering texture of sound
that was shot through with joy, on the day Armistice was declared.
Our tender sustained notes! Perfectly inflected whirlwinds!
We constructed a musical edifice out of shaped air
that evening, as if we were charged with high-voltage light.
We played chorus after chorus of "That Man of Mine" that night.

Don't Get It Twisted

Vi Burnside, Rosita Cruz, and Willie Mae Wong on Saxophones

We traveled to Europe, on a USO tour:
the cities still bombed-out, destroyed;
the people still shocked, in a nightmare awake.
Our job was to cheer up the boys.

We played to reduce their "Occupation Army Blues."
They were thousands of light-years away from home,
and things they had seen gave them inner armoring
and internal skies clouded with gloom.

Our quicksilver swing proved a reawakening:
lots of uniformed men learned again how to smile.
Our Sweethearts split time, in long melodic lines,
and the soldiers jitterbugged in the aisles.
Yes, they danced in the aisles!
The boys danced in the aisles.

Mercy, Mercy, Mercy

Julian "Cannonball" Adderley on Alto Sax

For many months I had lain unplayed in velvet,
my molecules contracting with cold, expanding with heat.
By the time I was held again I had almost forgotten
that the mystery of breath is concealed in every note.

My boy came home from war with a new ear for music:
new scales, new chords, new tempo, and new harmony;
a music as fragmented as those post-war times were,
a music for "The Age of Anxiety."*

Bebop was intricate, nervous, fast-paced, intense;
its enjoyment reached in quiet listening.
In it, popular music evolved beyond dance.
It was the birth of "cool," the beginning of the end of swing.

*1948 Pulitzer Prize for Poetry awarded to W. H. Auden's *The Age of Anxiety*.

IMPROVISATION, 1948*

JOHNNIE MAE RICE ON PIANO

(The piano remembers.)

(L) A heap of broken images.

                 (R) Equal and inalienable rights.

(L) So elegant, so intelligent.

                 (R) Recent barbarous acts.

The dead tree gives no shelter.

                 Freedom of speech and belief.
                 Freedom from fear and want.

The last fingers of leaf.
Fear in a handful of dust.
Hurry up, please, it's time.
And fiddle whisper music.

                 The conscience of mankind.
                 All members of the human family.
                 Inherent dignity.
                 A common standard of achievement.
                 All born free.
                 No one subject to torture
                 or degrading punishment.
                 Equal in dignity and rights.

Dry bones. The river's tent.   The right to seek asylum.
                 The right to a nationality.

Departed, have left no address.
Each in his prison thinks of the key.

*1948: From the United Nations, a Universal Declaration of Human Rights;
   Nobel Prize in Literature awarded to poet T. S. Eliot, author of "The Wasteland."

Drum Solo, 1950

Pauline Braddy on Drums

(The drum-kit remembers.)

Oh, the jukebox jamming
a recorded blare;
oh, the record player:
music everywhere.

Oh, the television,
oh, the brides and grooms,
oh, the male musicians.
Oh, the bare ballrooms.

Oh, the perfect family:
boy, girl, dog, home.
Oh, the undanced rhythms.
Oh, the atom bomb.

A klook a mop, a klook a mop: salt peanuts!
Ragamuffin, ragamuffin. Peach!

The Song Is You

Lucille Dixon on Bass

Musical instruments sleep in the dark
for several hours a day:
the folks we belong to aren't always at play,
so we can't be always at work.

Our silence holds music: an undiscovered bourne,
horizons which have never been viewed,
like undeclared love growing deeper in solitude,
or the crystalline heart of a stone.

My sleep, however, was more like a death:
in the dark of an attic for years;
forgetting my existence, and my glorious career
with the best female swing band on the earth.

I was the great love of my Sweetheart's life.
A man came between us. And soon
I was in the dark collecting dust and out of tune;
they were pronounced man and wife.

Instead of the charts, my gal read Dr. Spock.
We played once a week, once a year . . .
At first, from my closet, I was able to hear
her family's continuo of talk.

My Sweetheart's grandson brought me to the shop.
Something has ruined my voice.
Older, not riper, I'm a sorry old bass.
But that doesn't mean I've lost hope

. . .that someone will hold me in a tender embrace,
her arms will encircle my neck;
someone will press her warm length to my back,
and pluck notes from my gut with her fingers' caress.

Untitled Swing Instrumental

Arr. Eddie Durham

As performed by the World Famous International Sweethearts of Rhythm,

Under the Leadership of Anna Mae Winburn,

As Remembered by Several Old Band Instruments at Midnight in the Back Room

Of Lebeau's One-Stop Pawnshop, New Orleans, Louisiana

August 28, 2005

Darling, I'm so into you, Baby.
Darling, I'm so into you, Baby.
Darling, I'm so into you, Baby.
Darling, I'm so into you, Baby.
Darling, I'm so. Baby!
Honey, I'm so. Baby!
Darling, I'm so, darling, I'm so,
Darling, I'm so into you, Baby.
Darling, I'm so into you, Baby.

Baby, me, too, child! Babe, me, too, child!
Baby, me, too, Baby, me, too.
Baby, I'm so into you, Sweetheart.
Sweetheart, I'm so into you, Darling.
Darling, I'm so into you, Baby.
Darling, I'm so into you, Baby.
  (Keep repeating until daylight.)

The International Sweethearts of Rhythm: Chronology

1909

Laurence C. Jones founds the Piney Woods Country Life School in Piney Woods, Mississippi, for poor and orphaned African American children.

1937

Jones organizes an all-girl band of students from Piney Woods. Because the band includes a Chinese saxophonist, a Hawaiian trumpeter, and a Mexican clarinetist as well as African American musicians, he names them the International Sweethearts of Rhythm.

Chaperoned by Rae Lee Jones, the Sweethearts start touring to raise money for the school.

1939

The Sweethearts perform throughout the South and the Midwest.

Germany invades Poland. Great Britain and France declare war on Germany. World War II begins.

1940

The band breaks attendance records in cities across the United States, performing to sold-out and standing-room-only crowds.

1941

The Sweethearts sever ties with Piney Woods School (reasons vary), turn professional, and move to Arlington, Virginia. Rae Lee Jones is now their manager.

The band breaks box-office records at the Howard Theatre in Washington, D.C., drawing 35,000 people in a single week. They perform at the Apollo Theatre in Harlem and the celebrated Savoy Ballroom.

Japan attacks Pearl Harbor. The United States declares war on Japan. Germany and Italy declare war on the United States.

1942

New musicians are hired, including Anna Mae Winburn, who had fronted several male bands. She becomes the band's leader. Seasoned saxophonist Vi Burnside and trumpeter Tiny Davis join the band, which soon includes many of the best female musicians of the day.

The Sweethearts play in "battles of the sexes" against famous all-male organizations, including Fletcher Henderson's band. They tour major cities in their own $15,000 Pullman bus. They break all existing records at Chicago's Regal Theater, including those held by Count Basie and Louis Armstrong.

The U.S. government orders more than 110,000 Japanese American men, women, and children to leave their homes and detains them in remote, military-style camps.

U.S. troops arrive in Europe.

1943

Now known as the "Musical Novelty of the Century," the Sweethearts return to the Apollo in New York, then play sixty one-nighters across seven states. More than four thousand people stand in line on opening night of a weeklong run at the Palace Theatre in Memphis.

Trumpeter Toby Butler and saxophonist Roz Cron become the first white members of the band.

1944

The band is named "America's #1 All-Girl Orchestra" by *DownBeat* magazine.

On D-Day (June 6), the Allies land on the beaches of Normandy, France.

1945

The Sweethearts play for Armed Forces Jubilee Programs broadcast over short-wave radio to troops stationed overseas. In July, they sail to Europe for six months of shows with the USO. They play primarily for white U.S. soldiers.

The United States drops an atomic bomb on the city of Hiroshima in Japan. Three days later, a second nuclear bomb is detonated over Nagasaki.

Germany surrenders. Japan surrenders. World War II is officially over.

1946

The Sweethearts record four songs, two for RCA Victor and two for Guild Records. Some band members are tired of being on the road. Some leave to get married and begin other careers. The band's lineup changes.

The Big Band era comes to an end.

1947

Rae Lee Jones announces a European tour that never happens.

1949

Rae Lee Jones dies at the age of 49. The band folds. Few white jazz fans have ever heard their music.

1980

In March, fifteen former band members reunite at the Women's Jazz Festival in Kansas City, Missouri, which features a special Salute to the "Original" International Sweethearts of Rhythm.

AUTHOR'S NOTE

The International Sweethearts of Rhythm was a sixteen-piece big band that played swing music in the 1940s. A type of jazz, swing was the most popular music of the time, and hundreds of bands played it on the radio, in movies, in ballrooms and clubs. Two things set the Sweethearts apart: All of its musicians and its leader were women, and it was the first integrated all-women swing band in the world. Most of the band members were African American, but others were white, Chinese, Mexican, Native American, and Hawaiian. (Hawaii was not yet a state.)

To prepare for writing about the Sweethearts, I spent time at the library and online reading about them, watched a documentary film about them, and listened to as much of their music as I could find. I also listened to swing music by other famous big bands, including those led by Count Basie, Duke Ellington, Cab Calloway, Benny Goodman, Fletcher Henderson, Glenn Miller, and Fats Waller. I danced around the house a lot. I read memoirs by swing musicians and interviews with jazz musicians. I read Wynton Marsalis. I learned about the instruments the Sweethearts played: saxophone, trumpet, drums, trombone, bass. My brother, Mel Nelson, is a jazz musician, and he helped me understand more about the instruments and how they work. My friend Tim Moran, who plays woodwinds, walked me through "the ritual of the reed."

I studied the times in which the Sweethearts lived: the social, political, and world events happening around them. It was extremely difficult during the 1940s for female musicians to be taken seriously as jazz artists. One reason for the Sweethearts' success was that many male musicians were off serving in World War II. If Americans back home wanted to go out and hear music and dance and have a good time, they had to see the female bands, like the Sweethearts. They were surprised by how good the "gals" sounded and how hard they could swing.

The Sweethearts played to sold-out crowds of mostly black audiences in New York, Chicago, and Washington, D.C. They did not travel much in the Deep South because the band was integrated, which defied Southern "Jim Crow" laws. When they were in the South, they ate and slept on their private bus because black and white members of the band weren't allowed in the same restrooms, restaurants, and hotels. The white members of the band had to wear dark makeup and wigs on stage so they could pass as black; otherwise, the police would arrest them. It was illegal for black and white musicians to play together. They toured coast-to-coast in their bus and played "battle of the bands" concerts against some of the most famous big bands of the day. They became so famous that African American soldiers stationed overseas started letter-writing campaigns to bring the Sweethearts to Europe. In 1945, they became the first black women to travel there with the USO.

By 1949, the Big Band era was over, and so were the Sweethearts. The men had returned from the war and small-group bebop was the new sound of jazz. Women who had played in bands—and worked in other jobs like engineering, manufacturing, and the sciences—were asked to step aside so returning veterans could be re-employed. Only four members of the Sweethearts were able to continue working as musicians. Anna Mae Winburn, the band's former leader, started another band that lasted only a few years; she later worked as a domestic, cleaning houses. The Sweethearts were almost forgotten, except by people who had seen and heard them play, until the 1960s and 1970s, when the band was rediscovered by the feminist movement.

The poems in this book tell the Sweethearts' story. Since Jerry Pinkney and I had decided at the outset that each of us would do something in this book which we had never done before, I wrote the poems in "swingier" triple (anapestic and dactylic) meters, borrowing rhythms from several nineteenth-century poems I loved long ago, by Ralph Waldo Emerson, Henry Wadsworth Longfellow, Alfred Noyes, and Robert Louis Stevenson. And instead of having the Sweethearts speak, or having the poet (me) tell about them, I followed my brother Mel's suggestion that I write in the voices of the instruments. I imagined that all of the instruments the Sweethearts played—Tiny Davis's trumpet, Ina Bell Byrd's trombone, Roz Cron's tenor saxophone, Johnnie May Rice's guitar, Pauline Braddy's drums—had somehow ended up in the same pawnshop in New Orleans. The title of each poem is the name of a popular swing standard.

Imagine, if you can, the great pleasure of seeing my plain black-and-white words transformed into brilliantly colorful, layered visual images. From the battered saxophone case on the frontispiece through pictures suggesting the war, the internment camps, the nation's hunger for moments of simple joy, and the racism gnawing away at its viscera, the effect I had hoped my poems would achieve, of pulling readers into the historical period during which the Sweethearts played, is wonderfully fulfilled in Jerry's art.

It's the evening of August 28, 2005. The pawnshop owner has left for the day, locking the door behind him. The instruments begin sharing tales and memories of the "good old days." They discover that several of them were, at one time, played by the same band, and they reminisce about the musicians ("my girl," "my gal") who played them. Sometimes they disagree about the meaning of swing. (The guitar, having had an earlier career during the Great Depression, when it was played by a musician of protest—someone like Woody Guthrie—has especially strong opinions.) The night passes. History comes alive. Just before dawn, the instruments find a riff, a groove, a vamp they keep repeating. We leave them as the sun rises and Hurricane Katrina arrives.

Artist's Note

Sometime early in 2007 my publisher asked me if I would be interested in collaborating with the poet Marilyn Nelson. I jumped at the chance. For years I had respected and admired Marilyn's poetry. The two of us had met occasionally at literary conferences and I had hoped that someday we would work together.

I was further enticed by the project's subject matter. I have been interested in jazz since my teenage years, and was a member of my high school jazz club. To this day I am an avid collector of jazz recordings, and I have always felt that I'd like my art to look the way that music sounds.

Somehow I didn't know about the International Sweethearts of Rhythm, this all-girl swing band with so much historical value. I had heard, though, of the school where the group was formed, the Piney Woods Life School in Piney Woods, Mississippi. In fact, materials about that school were filed away in my home from a time in the 1990s when I had had some conversations about the school's progressive mission and the possibility of my visiting to speak with the young African American students there.

All the stars seemed to be in alignment for this project. When Marilyn Nelson and I spoke on the phone, sharing our thoughts and ideas, it was clear to both of us that there was enough material in the Sweethearts history from 1935–1945 to fill a book. The time in which their music was created was turbulent, yet this band brought joy to all ages.

With much anticipation, I waited to read the poems that Marilyn would author. I knew they would be crafted and articulated in a beautiful and powerful manner. However, I was not prepared for what I received. Her poems were in the voice of the instruments, both stunning and arresting in their delivery. Nevertheless, how was I going to visually interpret a story of an all-girl touring band, where the storytelling is done by a sax or drum? I immediately called Marilyn to express my excitement about her writing. I told her that I would treat her poetry, and my art, in a new way. It was easy to say at the time. Yet after thinking on it for some length, I had not the foggiest idea of what a new way would entail. What had I gotten into? I wondered.

I read Marilyn's poems over and over again, and finally realized that I had to just begin. So I got thumbnails and a book dummy onto the page, and gave them to Lauri Hornik and Lily Malcom, my editor and art director. At that first meeting we agreed on the page count and the general layout. Comments on my concept were forwarded to me. Then I began to work in earnest.

But the poems presented further challenges. They

were reading in a way other than the dummy-book concepts that I had submitted. My newest perspective on this project was less narrative than what I had previously thought. "Now what?" I asked myself.

The task, I decided, was to create illustrations that would convey the war and the Depression years, as well as the color and texture of the band's vibrant music. This music became a balm to all Americans. Hard times and joy would parallel each other in my art for this book, in soup kitchens and military enlistment lines, in dance halls and overseas military bases. I began to research this period in history with my assistant, Jesse Bourdon (without whom I could not have done this project).

Reading, sketching, gathering research, and more sketching—there was so much for me to mine from those traumatic years. Visualizing music had always been of interest to me. Over the years I had been collecting books on that subject. The use of color and collage in many of my library's images was striking. An idea came to me to use two voices, one overlaying the other. I would interpret the times: World War II, the Japanese internment camps, the Great Depression, the Dust Bowl, and Jim Crow. Then alongside it I would depict the Swing period.

Marilyn's poems were titled after the songs of the era.

My assistant found music sheets for one of those titles and photocopied them onto colored paper. The era was layered, the music was layered, the art needed to be layered. After two years of sketching, it all became clear. I needed to create my art as it had always been executed, then find a way to suggest the sound and magic of the music. I constructed a collage over my art with squares, different shapes of brilliant and textured colored papers, and torn pieces of the photocopied music sheets. Later, I began adding pieces from maps of the U.S. to suggest travel, and flowers to speak to the beauty found in the Sweethearts of Rhythm.

These young girls, through their talents, gifts, and grit, used the music of the time to uplift the spirits of their fellow Americans. Swing was the place and space where one could let go of the weights that everyone shouldered. The Sweethearts used the bandstand to reinforce American ideals by integrating its members at the time of Jim Crow. They spoke through their horns a message of hope, and beat out marching orders on their drums to resist the evils of intolerance and war. My hope is that this book will make readers revisit that time and be inspired by the tremendous contributions of the International Sweethearts of Rhythm.

The International Sweethearts of Rhythm: Bibliography

Film and Recordings

Big Band Jazz: The Jubilee Sessions, 1943 to 1946. Hindsight Records, 1996. ASIN B00000F1SG. Includes three songs by the Sweethearts: "Blue Lou," "Tuxedo Junction," and "Swing Shift."

International Sweethearts of Rhythm: America's Hottest All-Girl Band, a film by Greta Schiller and Andrea Weiss. 1986; 30 min. Available from Jezebel Productions. http://www.jezebel.org

The International Sweethearts of Rhythm: Hot Licks 1944–1946: Rare Recordings from One of the Best American All Girl Big Bands of the Swing Era. Sounds of Yesteryear, 2006. ASIN B000CPWCTU. A compilation of live radio appearances.

The Sweethearts Project. The Kit McClure Band. Red Hot Records, 2004. UPC 616892579724. UPC 181212000061. Original arrangements as performed by the International Sweethearts of Rhythm and reinterpretations of their music. Available from CD Baby. http://www.cdbaby.com
———. *Just the Thing: The Sweethearts Project Revisited.* The Kit McClure Band. Motema Records, 2006. UPC 181212000061. Available from CD Baby. http://www.cdbaby.com

Print

The International Sweethearts of Rhythm by D. Antoinette Handy (Scarecrow Press, 1983).

"The Ladies Who Swing the Band" by Nat Hentoff in *American Legacy: The Magazine of African-American History & Culture,* Summer 2008, pp. 40–47.

Swing Shift: "All-Girl" Bands of the 1940s by Sherri Tucker (Duke University Press, 2000).

"The Untold Story of the International Sweethearts of Rhythm" in *Marian McPartland's Jazz World: All in Good Time* by Marian McPartland (University of Illinois Press, 2002). Also in *Reading Jazz: A Gathering of Autobiography, Reportage, and Criticism from 1919 to Now* edited by Robert Gottlieb (Pantheon, 1996).

Web

"The International Sweethearts of Rhythm." Article by Susan Fleet, trumpeter, music historian, and novelist. http://archives.susanfleet.com/documents/isr-4-page.html

"The International Sweethearts of Rhythm." History of Washington Park, City of Charlottesville. http://www.charlottesville.org/Index.aspx?page=539

"The International Sweethearts of Rhythm." Tonea Stewart interviews Sweethearts saxophonist Rosalind Cron on *Swingtime: A One Hour Special for Black History Month 2008* from Artemis Media Project and Public Radio International. http://www.swingtimepublicradio.org/sweethearts.htm

"International Sweethearts of Rhythm: America's #1 All-Girl Band." *Riverwalk Jazz,* March 8, 2007. A salute to the band in honor of National Women's History Month featuring interviews with trombonist Helen Jones Woods and alto saxophonist Roz Cron and live air-checks from 1945–46. http://www.riverwalkjazz.org/site/PageServer?pagename =jazznotes_intl_sweethearts

"International Sweethearts of Rhythm—4 numbers (1946)." YouTube. http://www.youtube.com/watch?v=tpNjAmQmq90